Original title:
Life's Meaning: Currently Out of Stock

Copyright © 2025 Creative Arts Management OÜ
All rights reserved.

Author: Vivian Laurent
ISBN HARDBACK: 978-1-80566-176-4
ISBN PAPERBACK: 978-1-80566-471-0

Between the Lines of Existence

We search for wisdom at the mall,
But all we find is a rubber ball.
In aisle three, they claim it's key,
To know the secrets of you and me.

The clerk just shrugs, says, "Try again!"
I ask for purpose, he points to Zen.
But Zen, my friend, is out of stock,
So here we are, just counting clocks.

Whispers of the Unseen

I asked a cat about my plight,
He licked his paw, said, "Not tonight!"
The goldfish sighed, in swirling glee,
"You'll find your answers at half-past three!"

But when I checked, the clock was wrong,
With signs and signals, I'll sing a song.
The whispers float, then fade away,
As I misplace yet another day.

Catching Shadows in the Twilight

I chased a shadow 'round the bend,
It giggled softly, then said, "Friend!"
It made me trip, I fell with flair,
And laughed at me for being there.

I grabbed a net, tried to reclaim,
But shadows dance, it's all a game.
They winked and fled into the night,
Leaving me with nothing in sight.

Forsaken Roads of Discovery

I took a road less traveled by,
Found rubber ducks stacked to the sky.
"Join us!" they quacked, and all I could see,
Were toys instead of wisdom's decree.

I honked my horn, thought I was smart,
But the ducks just quacked, stealing my heart.
So I rode away in a bubble of fun,
Discovering nothing—no wisdom won.

The Paradox of Abundance

I bought a cornucopia, oh what a sight,
Filled with dreams of more, from morn till night.
Yet here I stand, searching for glee,
While my fridge is overflowing, sans any brie.

Chocolate fountains and endless pies,
But what 'tis all worth, when hunger defies?
A banquet galore, yet I feel so lost,
Is this feast of plenty, worth the cost?

My pantry's a kingdom, my diet a jest,
With endless options, I still feel unrest.
Oh, to have simplicity - a slice or two,
Instead, I feast on choices, what's a soul to do?

So here I am, with a grin so fixed,
In a world of plenty, I'm starved and mixed.
An absurd buffet, life's ironic thrill,
As I navigate this menu, with absolutely nil.

Shadows of Unwritten Dreams

I penned my thoughts on napkins with flair,
Spouting ideas like confetti in air.
Yet when I check the font, it's all a blur,
Did I write a novel or maybe a slur?

Dreams loom large, like shadows at dusk,
Yet they scatter like rabbits, oh what a husk.
In the library of hopes, nothing seems right,
Just misplaced bookmarks that keep me up at night.

I chase after visions, like cats chase their tails,
Trying to capture the winds and the gales.
Yet in the chaos and quirks of my dreams,
The only epitaph is laughter, it seems.

So I gather my whispers, let mirth take wing,
In the twilight of hopes, I'll dance and sing.
For shadows of dreams are not void, but spry,
As I stockpile my laughter, oh my, oh my!

Searching for the Solace of Emptiness

I roamed through alleyways of silent regret,
Where echoes of nothingness seemed to be set.
But all I found was a quirky old cat,
Who meowed reassurance, and that was that!

In corners of corners, I sought a reprieve,
Yet all I uncovered was dust and a sleeve.
Why seek the void when it's cluttered with stuff?
In a world full of nonsense, is 'enough' ever enough?

On park benches, I pondered, with chips by my side,
Contemplating the meaning while nothing would bide.
Was this slice of nothing a glorious snack?
Or perhaps an illusion, reality's hack?

So let the silence reign, let the blandness unfold,
In the humor of emptiness, there's gold to behold.
For solace, they say, is where laughter has staked,
And I found it in nothingness, happily baked!

Unraveled Threads of Desire

A tapestry woven with colors so bright,
Yet the threads are tangled in life's funny plight.
I pulled at a string, and my dreams unraveled,
It's a circus of wishes, where laughter traveled.

Desires like socks, mismatched and wild,
I chase after them, like a beguiled child.
Each whim a puppet, dancing amok,
While my life's sitcom laughs at my luck.

In a world of 'wants', oh so vast and complex,
My desires mock me like hard-nosed reflex.
As I untangle the yarn, they skip and they twirl,
Why does fulfillment feel like a never-ending swirl?

But rejoice for the chaos, the failing façade,
In this carnival ride, let's applaud the odd.
For desires will tickle the funny bone right,
As we laugh through the threads, till the morning light.

Beyond the Horizon of Hope

I searched for wisdom in the fridge,
But all I found was stale bread.
My hopes were hidden in the back,
Somewhere under the moldy spread.

A rainbow appears in my cereal,
Promises of joy in each crunch.
Yet reality's a soggy mess,
A sad, soggy breakfast brunch.

When dreams fall like socks from the dryer,
And wishes get caught in the lint,
I laugh at the circus inside,
Each day a ridiculous hint.

So here's to the chases we take,
To the joys that all feel like play.
In this cartwheel of daily spins,
We'll find our way, come what may!

Fragments of a Faded Dream

Once I had plans for a castle,
With dragons and gold scattered around.
But I tripped over a shoelace,
Now I live in a cardboard bound.

My dreams were once glittering bright,
Like stars I could grasp with one hand.
Yet here I am, snug on the couch,
With chips as my royal command.

The fairytale ended on page two,
While I turned to a sitcom next.
Here's to adventures that flop,
Each laugh echoes my texted hex.

So let's toast with our iced coffee cups,
To hopes that have taken a dive.
We're the jesters of our own fate,
In this circus, at least we'll survive!

The Dim Glow of Forgotten Aspirations

I set my sights on a big dream,
A rocket with flashy, bright paint.
But the launchpad was out of order,
And so here I sit, somewhat faint.

With aspirations like old takeout,
Leftovers stuck to the plate.
I wipe off the goo and I chuckle,
For success, it just might be late.

My goals feel like socks split apart,
Missing their partners, it seems.
Yet in this odd world I wander,
I find solace in mismatched themes.

So laugh with me at the absurd,
As we build castles from the dust.
In this funny place we are lost,
Finding joy is the only must!

Navigating the Desert of Emotion

I wandered through sands of regret,
Where camels wear shades made of gold.
Each step a tumble, a misstep,
And my heart's growing painfully bold.

I drank from a well of despair,
Expecting sweet tea, got salt instead.
Yet laughter echoes in the dry air,
As I ponder my life on this bed.

The cactus waved as I passed by,
With arms like the hugs I never got.
But maybe it's here, in this sandstorm,
I'll find what I thought I forgot.

So here's to the laughs in the storm,
And the beauty hidden in rough.
We'll dance through the dunes of our whims,
In this crazy land, we'll get tough!

Pages Yet to Be Turned

Unwritten tales on empty sheets,
Procrastination, oh what a feat!
The pen sits idle, in a comical way,
Just waiting for inspiration to play.

Coffee spills on hopes and dreams,
A messy desk, or so it seems.
Maybe tomorrow, a fortune will bloom,
Or maybe it's just my cluttered room.

Each day I ponder, what should I write?
How to rhyme with a sandwich bite?
A cat walks by, with a curious glance,
Perhaps the answer is in his prance.

In other news, socks are mismatched,
Oh look! The laundry's utterly hatched!
Thoughts are wandering, away they flit,
But for now, I'll just sit and commit.

When the Clock Stands Still

Tick-tock, oh where did it go?
The hands of time forgot to show.
I sit and wonder, in this endless loop,
Should I dance or join a soup group?

Frozen seconds, they're really strange,
This hourglass is taking its range.
Got a snack, it's not a crime,
Might as well savor this precious time.

My phone says 'buzz,' but it's not a call,
Just a reminder to laugh and sprawl.
Each moment's a chance, or so I'm told,
To find silly joy in moments bold.

As I wait for time to take a leap,
Dreams float by, not too deep.
Someday, I'll write or maybe bake,
For now, I'll nap and enjoy the break.

Glimpses Through the Keyhole of Tomorrow

Peeking through a tiny lens,
What's ahead? More twists and bends!
Future cookies or a pie?
Oh please, don't let it be a fly.

Forecast says it's looking bright,
Or is that just my kitchen light?
What to wear? A hat or some flair?
Tomorrow's fashion, a funny affair.

I spy with my little eye,
A cat on a skateboard just zooming by.
Will that be the norm, who can tell?
Or am I tripping? Oh, what the hell?

Each glance reveals a curious scene,
Perhaps I'll just join their routine.
Unlock the door to all that's unknown,
Even if it's just my afternoon scone.

The Lingering Scent of Potential

In the air, a whiff of "maybe,"
Like burnt toast from my old rabies.
What will I do with this chance in hand?
Perhaps a cake, or just a band?

Scented candles, are they too much?
Mixed aromas, a lucky touch!
Pineapple pizza on the stove,
Is that potential? I'm in the groove!

Dreams are rising like warm bread dough,
Fluffy and bright, just watch them grow.
Each moment's a scoop of ice cream fun,
So many colors, where to run?

So here I stand, a fragrance free,
Potential wafting, come and see!
Mixing laughs with a dash of zest,
In the end, I'll just take a rest.

The Alchemy of Fleeting Instants

In the kitchen of chaos, we whip up a cake,
With a pinch of regret and a dash of a break.
Time's a jokester, playing tricks on our eyes,
As laughter bubbles up like a soda surprise.

We chase the glimmers, like moths to a flame,
Only to find out they're just a cruel game.
Each giggle a treasure, each fumble a prize,
Who knew that this mess would make us so wise?

Imprints on the Sands of Time

Footprints washed out by the tide's silly dance,
Scribbles in the sand, not left to enhance.
We build our castles with laughter and fun,
But the waves have a plan, they're not quite done.

Tickling the shore with whispers so sweet,
We trip on our past, while it wags a retreat.
In the surf's frothy grip, we tumble and roll,
Searching for secrets that water can't hold.

Unanswered Letters in a Drawer

There's a stack of letters I dare not unfold,
Each one a story just waiting to be told.
They sit with their secrets, a laugh trapped inside,
Like socks in a dryer, in a mysterious ride.

I ponder their contents, as dust bunnies play,
Perhaps they're love notes or bills that won't stay.
Yet still, they remain in their cozy old nest,
As I sip on my coffee, avoiding all the rest.

Dancing with the Ghosts of Ambition

I twirl with the phantoms of dreams left behind,
In a disco of doubts where the fog's not so kind.
With each step I take, they whisper and tease,
'You thought we had plans? Just dance with ease!'

The mirrors reflect every chance that I missed,
Yet still I keep spinning, wrapped in the mist.
For in this mad jig, there's a rhythm to find,
Laughter's the beat that can lighten the bind.

Pages Torn from the Book of Time

Once I found an old diary,
Full of doodles and spaghetti.
It said, 'Do what feels right,
But first, check your pantry.'

Each page turned, a new surprise,
Like socks lost—where do they hide?
I learned to laugh at the clock,
Time's a joker, oh what a ride!

Sometimes it's a puzzle, a game,
Where sanity sits in the back row.
Forget the why—just blame the cat,
For stealing the last piece of dough.

So here I sit with my quips,
Enjoying the chaos with glee.
Who needs a plan when you have snacks?
Let's toast with tea and a degree!

The Map to Nowhere

I've got a map marked with X's,
Each leads to a chocolate store.
But when I look for the treasure,
I'm left with a belly that's sore!

On my way to find wisdom,
I detoured to grab some fries.
The sign said, "Just take a left!"
But the left was full of lies.

Every fork in the road leads,
To leads to a new place to eat.
So I'll follow my hunger,
For that's one journey with treats!

In the end, I embrace the wrong,
With a grin and a burger in hand.
It's not about where I planned,
But the joy of a snack—oh so grand!

When Questions Fill the Room

Why do we dance when it rains?
Is it to avoid getting wet?
Why do the dogs chase their tails?
Answers? Not in this little vet!

What's the secret to a happy sock?
Do they prefer to go solo or pair?
And why won't my goldfish talk back?
He's got secrets he'll never share.

As questions float up like balloons,
I grab one and let out a cheer.
For every mystery unraveled,
Is just a laugh—and maybe a beer!

So here's to the questions we pose,
Riddles wrapped in pastry dough.
Let's roll with the absurdity,
And watch as the giggles unfold!

The Weight of Unsung Sonnets

These sonnets sit heavy on shelves,
Dusty dreams tucked in the cracks.
Each verse a weightless wish,
Yet somehow, they all relax!

I attempted to write something grand,
But ended up rhyming with cats.
My stanzas turned into a joke,
Now puns are where my heart's at.

Poets with pens like scepters,
Strutting like kings in the breeze.
Meanwhile, I juggle my snacks,
Grateful for crumbs and some cheese!

So let's raise a toast to our woes,
To ballads that never will sing.
For laughter's the song we all need,
With a twist on the everyday fling!

When the Price Tag Disappears

A shoe without a price is free,
But do I wear it, wait and see?
I tried to run, but lost a lace,
Now I'm just a joke in space.

With tags all gone, it feels absurd,
Like buying dreams without a word.
I asked the clerk for wisdom's cost,
She laughed and said, "You're already lost!"

Stickers flew like birds on high,
When discounts vanish, oh my my!
I pondered if it's worth the fuss,
As neighbors whispered, 'What's the plus?'

So here I stand, no cash, no clue,
A dance of thoughts in a shopping queue.
Not everything that's priced is gold,
Sometimes it's just a tale retold.

Ciphers in the Empty Room

In a room where echoes play,
I search for sense, but it's in decay.
Questions hang like cobwebs near,
While laughter's ghost is all I hear.

A riddle scrawled upon the wall,
Says, 'Finding truth is quite the haul.'
I scratched my head, then scratched my back,
Is clarity the thing I lack?

Chairs in corners sit and stare,
While couches breathe a stale old air.
I asked the table for some clues,
It just replied with creaks and snooze.

A clock without hands ticks unseen,
As time evades where I have been.
Ciphers dance like shadows spry,
And here I am, a wondering sigh.

Faded Signs of Forgotten Journeys

Once a route that promised sights,
Now it's lost to starry nights.
The signs have faded, rusted through,
Where did the thrills and good times strew?

These paths I took, now overgrown,
With whispers of the seeds I've sown.
I bumped into a road named 'Why?'
It laughed and waved, said 'Don't be shy!'

Maps that once exacted dreams,
Now navigate through silent screams.
I reached a fork that had no choice,
And listened hard for wisdom's voice.

Imaginary roads all weave,
Yet open eyes just make me grieve.
The journeys blur like watercolor,
In the end, we just need color.

Transactions of the Spirit

In the ongoing sale of my soul,
What's the value of feeling whole?
I haggled hard with hopes and fears,
But all they gave were stale souvenirs.

I brought my heart to the marketplace,
An awkward smile across my face.
The clerk just laughed and said, 'My friend,
Such treasures can't be bought or penned!'

With tokens made of dreams I find,
I barter with the threads of mind.
But every deal has its own price,
I'll take a smile, but not the vice.

Though spirits dance in quirky guise,
I'd trade a frown for clearer skies.
In this bazaar of heart and soul,
I'll laugh away while I take a stroll.

Windows Closed Against the Wind

When the breeze brings whispers loud,
I check each crack, I seal it proud.
Yet laughter rolls in, a playful guest,
Who knew my windows weren't the best?

The storm outside is quite a show,
But inside here, I've got a glow.
With cushions piled and snacks galore,
Who needs the wind if you've got more?

Each gust that rattles at my door,
Brings jokes and quirks to make me roar.
So let it howl and let it moan,
My happy fortress, all my own.

I raise a cup to tempest's wail,
With every chuckle, I set sail.
For in this room, I twist and spin,
With giggles loud, let the fun begin.

Strands of Thought in a Tangle

My mental strings are all a mess,
Like spaghetti dressed in fancy dress.
I tried to find some grand insight,
But tangled thoughts just caused a fight.

I pull one thread, it leads to snacks,
And then I'm lost in tasty tracks.
Each noodle leads me round and round,
Where wisdom's lost, but munchies found.

I plan a thought; it drifts away,
To daydreams bright of sunny play.
With every twist, the laughter grows,
Who cares if logic never shows?

So here I sit, my mind unspooled,
In goofy dance, I've been the fooled.
Yet with each turn, a chuckle blooms,
In tangled thoughts, joy always looms.

Emptiness in a Cupboard of Expectations

I opened up that cupboard wide,
Expectations stacked, a serious tide.
But all I found was dust and air,
And thoughts that danced without a care.

Where recipes of life were meant to be,
Instead, I found an empty spree.
I rummaged through with quite a hope,
Only to find a broken rope.

Old aspirations in layers thick,
But laughter was my little trick.
I squeaked and laughed, what a surprise,
Those empty shelves saw my joy rise.

So here I'll stay, with grins a song,
In cupboards bare, where I belong.
For nothing's better than to gleefully sift,
Through expectations that never lift.

The Abandoned Canvas of Dreams

My canvas stands all wide and bare,
With splashes missed and strokes of air.
I dipped my brush; it slipped away,
Yet bright ideas love to play.

Each stroke could tell a tale of cheer,
But I just smiled; there's nothing here!
With polka dots and vibrant sighs,
Leftover hopes wear funny ties.

I pondered colors, hues of glee,
Yet sketched a cat who climbed a tree.
With swirling shapes and splotches wide,
I laughed so hard my heart couldn't hide.

Abandoned dreams? Oh, just a jest,
In every blank, there's room for zest.
So here I dance with laughter's beam,
On my fine blank canvas of a dream.

Threads of Longing in a Frayed Edge

When I search for wisdom in my sock,
A missing mate is all I unlock.
Chasing threads that lead me awry,
Yet here I sit, and just ask why.

With every thought, a snag, a pull,
My quest for meaning feels so dull.
A fabric torn, yet still I weave,
In the chaos, I still believe.

Each lost connection tugs at my mind,
The answer's lost, nowhere to find.
Threads pulling tight, then letting go,
Fashion statements in life's grand show.

So here's to frays and tangled threads,
I'll wear my quirks like hats on heads.
With laughter stitched across my chest,
I'll find my joy—at least, a jest.

In Pursuit of Fleeting Moments

I chase the sunsets on my bike,
But all I catch is a silly hike.
With every blink, a moment flies,
While I search for answers in the skies.

The clock shakes its head, I sprint and dash,
But memories slip away like cash.
When life's a game and I'm just a pawn,
I laugh and run until the dawn.

Capture joy within a jar,
Yet all I find's an old candy bar.
Sweetness gone but laughter remains,
In silly times or silly gains.

So onward I go, with a goofy grin,
Chasing the moments I cannot win.
With each misstep, I find delight,
In the race of days from morn to night.

Filling the Void with Questions

Why does toast always land face down?
With every crunch, I wear a frown.
I ponder deeply on missing thoughts,
And fill my empty space with knots.

What's the purpose behind a sneeze?
Or why do socks love to take leave?
The fridge hums softly, a wise sage,
Yet answers seem like a blank page.

In search of truths, I eat dessert,
Chocolate cake makes the mind alert.
Questions swirl like a whipped cream dollop,
And I sip on joy till I want to stop.

Oh, fill the void with quirks and fun,
For life's a riddle, yet I have won.
In every query, laughter seeds,
And through sweet chaos, a heart still feeds.

The Silence of Untapped Potentials

In the corner sits my grand plan,
Gathering dust like a forgotten fan.
Whispers of dreams I've left unheard,
When I could soar like a funny bird.

Each hope a note in a silent song,
Yet here I am, where I don't belong.
With aspirations hiding in the shade,
I chuckle softly at plans I've laid.

I could juggle or dance, or so they say,
But I trip on thoughts and lose my way.
With every 'what if' I almost dive,
In awkward silence, I feel alive.

So here's to dreams that never bloom,
Sitting in corners, like dust in a room.
I'll laugh at the silence, I'll giggle and cheer,
For untapped potentials can still bring me near.

Colliding with the Unknown

I searched my pockets for the truth,
But all I found were faded receipts.
A fortune cookie missed the point,
It just served me some stale sweets.

I asked a squirrel for some advice,
He chattered back, then scurried away.
Turns out even critters have a life,
That doesn't involve my wild display.

I tried to peek behind the clouds,
Hoping for hints from stars above.
But they just blinked, as if to say,
"We're busy here, go find some love."

In the end, I danced with doubt,
Stumbled on some misplaced fun.
Sometimes the joke is on the seeker,
When absurdity outshines the run.

Conversations with the Silent Heart

I had a chat with my heart one night,
It whispered back with a silent grin.
I asked it why it felt so light,
It shrugged and said, "Just dive in!"

We pondered deep over cups of tea,
But the kettle whistled, gave us a fright.
"Is it wisdom or caffeine?" I asked,
It winked and said, "Both feel just right."

The toaster chimed in with a toast,
Said, "Burned slices tell their own tale."
In a world that eats its words fast,
I laughed and said, "What a hilarious fail!"

We made a pact to laugh more loud,
And coax the shadows into the light.
For in the giggles and in the grins,
There's something special in their flight.

The Fragments of an Elusive Truth

I found some puzzle pieces in my dreams,
Yet none of them fit quite the same.
Each one promised to reveal things,
But left me only with a silly game.

A dictionary taunted from the shelf,
With definitions I could not quite see.
I asked it, "Can you help?" It laughed,
"Sorry friend, I'm on a coffee spree!"

My mirror reflected a puzzled face,
It winked back with a smirk aligned.
"Searching for wisdom is a funny chase,
But maybe you just need more wine?"

As I gather fragments onto a plate,
I realize the search brings me cheer.
The elusive truth may just be this:
A smirk and a giggle is what we hold dear.

Searching for Signs in Empty Spaces

I wandered through some empty plots,
Looking for signs like a scavenger hunt.
Each rusty nail and broken pot,
Whispered echoes of some distant front.

The mailbox stood, with rusting charm,
Promising letters wrapped in delight.
I peeked inside, no note to disarm,
Just an old sock—what a funny sight!

I scanned the sky for messages learned,
Clouds just floated, blissful and free.
Maybe I'm chasing what's not returned,
While stars above wink knowingly.

In vacant lots and silence found,
I trip on bits of the playful past.
And often it's here, where laughter is bound,
That signs of joy come shining fast.

Reflections in an Abandoned Mind

Mirror, mirror, where's the glow?
Thoughts are wandering, just like a show.
Chasing shadows, where did they run?
Did I misplace my brain for fun?

Rummage through the corners dark,
Find my sanity, or just a spark.
Plans I had, not even a trace,
Did I leave them all at outer space?

Doodles on the walls so bright,
Trying to bring back the lost light.
But laughter echoes, what a tease,
In my head, it's just a breeze!

So here I sit, with thoughts like cats,
Chasing tails and wearing hats.
A circus show, all on my own,
In this mind, I'm never alone!

The Archive of Forgotten Dreams

Dusty shelves of what could be,
Dreams stacked high, a sight to see.
Once bold visions, now turned to mist,
Did I forget, or just resist?

Folders labeled, 'Maybe Someday',
Filled with hopes that went astray.
Colorful whims in a gray world,
Who knew this chaos would unfurl?

Tickle the archives, pull a file,
Find a wish that wears a smile.
But wait, what's that? An empty sheet,
Guess I lost it 'neath my feet!

A treasure hunt inside my head,
Finding giggles instead of dread.
Who needs plans or clever schemes?
Let's just laugh at shattered dreams!

Fables of the Unwritten

Pages blank, a writer's fright,
Words are hiding, take to flight.
Once I dreamed of tales so grand,
Now I'm left with empty hand.

Characters dance on the edge of thought,
But in this game, they're all for naught.
Plot twists wander off alone,
Where's the fun in writing stone?

Bind my stories with some cheer,
Laugh at schemes that disappear.
Each scribble holds a secret game,
Maybe I'll just draw a name!

Yet here I sit, a pen in tow,
With blankness causing quite the show.
But every laugh is worth a page,
In this fable of the sage!

Underneath the Surface of What Is

Plunge below the shallow tide,
Where nonsense and giggles often hide.
Waves of chaos, splashes of fun,
Diving deep, who needs a gun?

Snorkel in a sea of jest,
To find the heart that beats with zest.
Oh look, a fish with shoes so bright,
What a world devoid of fright!

Amidst the bubbles and silly sighs,
Lies the truth in goofy ties.
Strip away the serious bit,
And find the joy that won't quite fit.

As I float in the currents wide,
Laughing with the fish, I glide.
For what's beneath the playful guise,
Is where the sweetest laughter lies!

Echoes of Unfulfilled Purpose

In the cupboard of dreams, dust settles tight,
Each promise forgotten, just out of sight.
I went looking for answers, found mismatched socks,
Turns out my wisdom's just a pair of rocks.

Chasing big visions on a tricycle ride,
With a map full of scribbles, I can't seem to glide.
A treasure map leading right to the fridge,
Hungry for meaning, but still on the ridge.

I asked the wise owl, perched high in a tree,
He hooted and flapped, said, "Just let it be!"
So I logged onto dreams and hit 'update',
Now I'm waiting for life to call me on a date.

So here's to the journey, with giggles and sighs,
With pizza and laughter, and questionable fries.
For when purpose eludes me, I laugh with my pals,
In the circus of nonsense, I'm juggling my gals.

When Value Runs Dry

I checked my emotions in a yard sale spree,
Some were half price, and some were quite free.
I tried to pay in giggles, but they took my frown,
The value of joy seems to tumble down.

I ran to the market for wisdom and wit,
The shelves were all bare, not a thought left to split.
I bartered with hope for a smidgen of cheer,
But the clerk just chuckled and disappeared.

I scoured the internet for everything grand,
Searching for purpose from a digital stand.
But the Wi-Fi was sluggish, no answers in sight,
Just cat videos dancing through the dark of the night.

So I'll toast to the moments that don't come with tags,
With popcorn and soda in colorful rags.
When value runs dry, I'll just sip on my dreams,
And laugh with the universe's mysterious schemes.

In Pursuit of Whispers

I chased after whispers in the wind's soft hum,
Like a cat on a laser, oh where do they come?
I stumbled on echoes, a giggle or two,
But the secrets they held were just lost in the glue!

My heart became restless, a treasure map mess,
Pursuing those whispers led to a big press.
I asked the fairies if they'd lend me a clue,
They tangled up laughter and flew straight through.

I danced with the shadows under the full moon,
Searching for meaning in a comical tune.
But the more that I sought, the sillier it felt,
Like a big bag of jellybeans that never quite melted.

Yet in all this madness, joy spun in a twirl,
Finding bliss in the nonsense, life's playful whirl.
For in pursuit of whispers, I learned here tonight,
That the funny old journey is my sweetest delight.

Inventory of the Heart

I opened my heart like a thrift shop's display,
Full of forgotten dreams and a quirky ballet.
Sifting through laughter and a few lonely tears,
I marked down the smiles stacked high in frontiers.

There's a shelf for the silly, a drawer for the wise,
With puns and dad jokes all wrapped up in ties.
I counted my treasures, mixed joy with a dash,
Cataloging moments that went by in a flash.

I listed my hopes with a crayon so bold,
Stuck on a fridge that's now well-loved and old.
My inventory swells with the friends that I've met,
In this magical store, there's no need for regret.

So if you stop by, please check out the art,
The giggles and wonders that fill up my heart.
We'll all share a laugh as we trade our delight,
In this inventory, it's the smiles that take flight.

Shadows of What Could Have Been

Once dreamed of grandeur on a whim,
But now I'm lost in the last dim.
I ponder the paths not taken,
While munching snacks, blissfully awakened.

They say regrets make you grow wise,
Yet here I am, with pizza and fries.
With echoes of plans that slipped away,
I laugh them off like a quirky play.

In shadows where wishes play hide and seek,
I invite my old dreams, but they're growing bleak.
A future that promised all kinds of fun,
Now flops around like a fish out of run.

Yet here we sit, with laughter and cheer,
Counting "what ifs" like tips of a deer.
Though out of stock, let's stay in demand,
And dance in the light with a pizza in hand.

Navigating the Empty Corridors

I wandered through halls of what should've been,
Found echoes of laughter, but no hearty grin.
Each door I tried was a locked-up tease,
Whispering tales of my forgotten keys.

Down corridors painted a pastel hue,
Searching for meaning in a lost shoe crew.
I tripped on a memory just the other day,
Fell straight on my dreams in a comical way.

With every bend I would stop and sway,
Caught in the web of a grand café.
But all I found were crumbs and stains,
And a vending machine that played silly games.

So I roam on, giggling at the sights,
These empty corridors of whimsical bites.
Embracing the folly, I take pride as I tread,
In a quest for the snacks, not the thoughts in my head.

The Unraveled Fabric of Being

Threads of existence woven with care,
Tangled and twisted, isn't it rare?
Sweaters unravel when worn just right,
But mine's a jigsaw that won't fit tight.

I tried stitching dreams with the finest of thread,
Yet somehow ended up tucking in bread.
Cooked up plans that simmered away,
Lost in a stew that refused to play.

The seams of tomorrow fray in the light,
Each patch a joke, oh what a sight!
A fabric so wild, it laughs and twirls,
As I wear it proudly, amidst my swirls.

So here's my garment of mishaps and threads,
Dancing in circles as the world shreds.
With buttons missing but sparkles in place,
I strut down the lane with a goofy grace.

Traces of a Future Unseen

In the garden of dreams where futures mold,
I find weeds growing, brave and bold.
Each sprout a promise, a prank in disguise,
Taunting my senses with mischievous lies.

I wander 'neath skies of whimsical blue,
Collecting the footprints of folks who flew.
They trail off laughing, like echoes of fun,
Leaving me puzzled as I chase the sun.

Maps of tomorrow scribbled in sand,
Shift with the tides, slipping from hand.
"Maybe I'll meet what's waiting for me,"
Or just grab some cookies and take it easy.

So I'll bask in the beauty of whims that roam,
With traces of futures that feel like home.
With a chuckle and grin, I embrace the unknown,
For every lost path is a chance to have grown.

The Forgotten Symphony of the Heart

In a concert hall where silence reigns,
The heart forgot its playful gains.
No notes to play, just echoes free,
A dance of jest, a comedy.

With every beat, a joke untold,
Of love from ages young and old.
The maestro left to chase a snack,
While laughter echoes in the back.

Each thump a bongo, each thud a drum,
A symphony of nonsense, here it's come.
The audience waits, but all they hear,
Is the sound of someone spilling beer.

So raise a glass to all that's missed,
In life's grand play, a funny twist.
Between the music, laughs entwine,
In the heart's chorus, that's just fine.

Breaths Held in Anticipation

I held my breath for quite a spell,
Waiting for meaning, but who can tell?
A cat passed by, meowed its tease,
While I just sat, a frozen breeze.

The clock ticked slow, like molasses' song,
Anticipation, but what's wrong?
A pizza pie, a sudden chime,
I gasped for meaning in my prime.

The doorbell rang, I jumped a mile,
Was it the truth or just a smile?
Wrong package, just socks and cheese,
I sighed and laughed, oh, life's unease.

Who needs the secrets wrapped in style?
When waiting's just part of the trial.
I took a breath, let laughter creep,
In the silence, a joke does deep.

The Garden of Unplanted Seeds

In a garden plot, I dreamed of blooms,
But I forgot to plant, just gloomy fumes.
Weeds take over, a green brigade,
My life's a joke, an unmade grade.

Each seed a thought of what could be,
But I just sat, with my cup of tea.
Sunshine bright but not for me,
In my mind's garden, all lies free.

A tumbleweed rolled, my idea's fall,
With giggles echoing, the garden's call.
I watered weeds, gave them a name,
But deep down, it's all just a game.

So here's to seeds that never sprout,
In this garden filled with doubt.
I'll raise a spade to what was lost,
And laugh at all it cost and cost.

The Haunting of Unlived Lives

Ghosts of plans float through the air,
Whispers of dreams that went nowhere.
I see the "what-ifs" poke their heads,
In a haunted house, where laughter spreads.

The party's on, yet I just stare,
At shadows twisting without a care.
Each missed chance, a quirky ghost,
Dancing around like they know the most.

They knock on wood, they knock on dreams,
In spectral fun, or so it seems.
Yet here I stand with snacks and sighs,
Grabbing popcorn as a ghostly surprise.

So let's toast to lives yet led,
To laughter's haunt, to dreams unsaid.
In haunted halls where humor thrives,
We'll celebrate these ghostly lives.

Empty Boxes and Forgotten Dreams

In a cupboard stacked with hopes,
I found a box marked 'Do Not Open'.
Inside, the dreams of yesterday,
Are gathered dust, quietly broken.

The labels peel, the colors fade,
It's like a yard sale of my mind.
Are those my goals or just a charade?
Who knew my dreams were so hard to find?

I sift through wishes, all askew,
A toy or two from happier days.
I chuckle softly, who knew it true?
Hope is a game of jumbled plays.

So here I sit, with boxes galore,
Searching for joy in a cardboard box.
Why did I think I'd find something more?
Turns out it's only a big paradox.

The Search for What Eludes Us

On a scavenger hunt, my map is wrong,
X marks the spot but there's just a frown.
I check everywhere, I sing my song,
But all I find is the cat rolling down.

Like lost socks in the dryer's whirl,
What's gone missing? I'm quite perplexed.
Is it wisdom, or just a pearl?
Or maybe the remote? So vexed!

I consult the oracle of my snooze,
Awake at midnight with playful thoughts.
"Can I trade this in for better news?"
But all I get are the same old knots.

But hey, let's dance with what we've found,
A broccoli stick and an old shoe lace.
In this quest for what's not around,
I'll dance like there's no empty space!

Lost In the Inventory of Existence

I walked the aisles of my own mind,
With shopping carts of fleeting notions.
Each shelf holds wonders that I can't find,
A circus of forgotten emotions.

Did I order courage, or just a snack?
A tower of dreams leaned, and then fell.
I reach for hope, but it's out of whack,
The price tag on joy? Hard to tell.

I check the clearance for self-esteem,
Two for one on all my regrets.
A coupon for laughter? Just a dream,
As I ponder these silly debts.

So here I am, a bargain shop knave,
With thoughts more tangled than a maze.
I chase the whims that I try to save,
And find humor in this quirky phase.

The Shelves are Bare

I walked to the store of grand ideas,
But all I see are empty racks.
No wisdom left, just lingering fears,
No life hacks or quirky little facts.

The stockroom is bare, it's quite a sight,
I'm left with lists of things I can't seek.
What should I buy to feel alright?
Perhaps a good laugh, or a brand-new streak?

No self-help books, no guide on trends,
Just a mirror that reflects my plight.
Shopping for joy with all my friends,
But their humor's dimmed by the lack of light.

So I leave the store, with nothing in hand,
Except a chuckling heart and a grin.
Let's toast to the void—oh isn't it grand?
The shelves may be bare, but the fun's not thin!

Hues of an Overcast Day

Gray skies above, a canvas so bland,
With puddles reflecting, our plans went unplanned.
A squirrel in a tux, raiding a bin,
Laughing at sunshine, for where has it been?

A dance in the rain, or a slip on the mat,
Jokes piled like laundry, where's my old hat?
Who needs a rainbow when clouds bring the cheer?
Just call the weatherman, seems winter's still here!

Lemonade stands closed, it's soup that we seek,
A grin in the gloom, who said gray cannot speak?
Each droplet a whisper of humor in trees,
Tickling our worries, oh yes, if you please!

Yet in all the gray, colors blur and collide,
Resilience a palette, with joy as our guide.
So here's to the overcast, the drizzle today,
Let's paint with our laughter, and lighten the gray!

Searching for the Echo of a Song

In a room full of echoes, I hum offbeat,
Searching for lyrics, can't find my own seat.
The radio's broken, the cat's in a funk,
I serenade shadows, meet up with a junk!

Laughter is missing, I friend my own rhyme,
Yet the fridge joyfully chimes, it's snack time!
Though rhythms elude on this curious quest,
Who needs Top Forty, when leftovers are best?

The chorus I miss is replaced by a snore,
As spoons start a symphony, tapping the floor.
A grand waltz with forks—oh how they spin!
Searching for music, I'll start with my kin!

In the silence, there's magic, it dances around,
Life's silly serenades, with humor abound.
So I'll jive with my cat, let the toaster take part,
For every dish has a tune—just don't lose your heart!

Time's Faded Inscription

Tick-tock whispers, the clock plays its game,
Counting the seconds, but who's really to blame?
With each tiny tick, I'm late for my tea,
Can these hours pretend they're just marching for me?

Last week feels like ages, today's lost in a fog,
Like pants that have shrunk, oh my, what a slog!
Yet here in the chaos, I giggle and muse,
For time's just a jester, with nothing to lose!

A schedule in tatters, my plans turn to dust,
But laughter's the remedy, oh yes, it's a must.
Forget all the deadlines, be merry and bright,
With jokes on the calendar, the future feels light!

So grab your old watch and toss it away,
Let's dance to the rhythms of silly foray.
In moments unmeasured, we'll frolic and cheer,
For time's just a prankster, let's give it a sneer!

Dreams Shelved for Another Day

Dusty are dreams on a shelf stacked high,
Waiting for magic, or maybe a try.
Plans made last Tuesday? None followed through,
And yet here I am, with a sip of cold brew!

Procrastination's fun, like a cat on a chair,
Ignoring my to-do list, like it just isn't there.
Cereal for dinner, who needs gourmet?
When dreams take a nap, they still find a way!

With clouds for my pillow, I drift into schemes,
Each one a giggle, a wish, or a meme.
Oh, the joy in the waiting, in dreams left to play,
For laughter's the fuel that brightens the gray!

So here's to the dreams that don't always arrive,
Accompanied by puns, they start to come alive.
With humor as wisdom, let's pack up and stray,
For dreams shelved for later are still here to stay!

The Echo of Unanswered Questions

In a world of endless chatter,
I send my queries on a platter.
But echoes laugh and fade away,
Leaving me puzzled, led astray.

The sofa groans with heavy sighs,
While my goldfish ponders why.
A box of cereal waits to speak,
But wisdom seems so far, so bleak.

I ask the moon about my fate,
It twinkles back—it's running late.
The fridge hums tunes of mystery,
Who knew it held such history?

I chase the shadows, dance with doubt,
With every giggle, scream, and shout.
For answers swirl like autumn leaves,
And tease me with their web of weaves.

Echoes of an Empty Shelf

Once on a shelf, wisdom lay,
Till dust bunnies took it away.
Now jars and cans stare at me,
Their secrets kept, oh woe is me!

The soap suds giggle in delight,
While fries debate their fate tonight.
Each can of beans has much to say,
But none can find the words today.

I've turned the shelf upside down,
No nuggets of truth to be found.
Just a spoon that's lost its partner,
And a can opener, worse than a charlatan.

In this cupboard, silence reigns,
While the ketchup bottle complains.
I sit, marooned in thought's abyss,
All I wanted was knowledge—what a miss!

The Search for Whispered Truths

In corners dim, the secrets hide,
Behind the curtain, truth denied.
I tiptoe through this quirky maze,
In search of whispers from the days.

The dog barks loudly, what a tease!
He claims he knows just where to squeeze.
But chasing tails leads me in loops,
And I end up just with fuzzy snoops.

The cat sits high with knowing eyes,
She smirks at my bewildered sighs.
With every leap, she knows the score,
While I'm left pondering 'what's in store?'

Battling socks, trolls on the floor,
The vacuum cleaner isn't a bore.
Yet still I trot humanly forth,
In search of truth that defines my worth!

Reflections in a Dusty Mirror

I glance at the mirror, covered in grime,
It shows ragged thoughts, unfit for prime time.
With each smudge and smear, I blink and stare,
What wisdom lies hidden within such a glare?

It laughs at my hair that's gone awry,
Reflecting mishaps you just can't deny.
What lessons can come from a tangled mess?
Except maybe that I ought to dress less!

Behind the grime, a truth seems to glow,
Perhaps it's just coffee stains; who really knows?
I ponder my fate while fixing my tie,
Though clearly, my shirt looks like it's ready to cry.

But still I strut, with mirror in tow,
Twirling my thoughts in a zany row.
For laughter and joy are the mirrors of heart,
Reminding me how fun this life can start!

When Stars Fail to Shine

When the sun took a nap, the stars fell asleep,
They missed their cue, their promises to keep.
The sky's the limit, but not when it's night,
Do they hide in the clouds, or just run from the light?

The moon cracked a joke, but no one could hear,
It echoed through darkness, then disappeared.
Astrologers puzzled, lost in their charts,
They shuffled the stars like a pack of old cards.

We're wishing on wishes that didn't arrive,
Sipping on stardust, trying to thrive.
But laughter erupts from the cosmic jest,
Stars may be shy, but they're still our best guest.

So here's to the nights when the stars stay away,
We'll dance with the shadows, come what may!
With giggles and grins, let's toast to the skies,
For even in silence, the fun never dies.

Searching for Light in the Depths

In a world full of shadows, I search for a beam,
Hoping to catch a glimmer or dream.
I checked the fridge, thought it might glow,
But all I found was an old veggie row.

Tried turning on lamps, but they flickered away,
Even the candles plucked up their play.
The cat's in the corner, with eyes all aglow,
I asked for some guidance, but she's stealing the show.

Stumbling through chaos, I roam and I roam,
Catching lost thoughts in a jar labeled 'home'.
Yet light's just a concept when the fridge makes a hum,
And laughter erupts from the depth of the dumb.

But who needs a spotlight when silliness reigns?
In darkness we giggle, through joy and through pains.
So grab the nearest shadow, and twirl it about,
For searching for light is what life's all about!

A Breath Between Destinies

Here's a thought wrapped tight in a smile,
Between breaths of fate, let's linger awhile.
We chase after choices, like cats on the run,
Yet every wrong turn brings more jests to our fun.

The universe giggles at our frantic pace,
As we trip over dreams, yet still find our space.
There's humor in stumbles, grace in the fall,
So let's laugh at the chaos, embrace it all.

Like juggling planets with a sneeze and a cough,
The absurdity flows, as we take off the cloth.
And while we ponder on what's next in our quest,
Let's savor each moment, and forget all the rest.

For each breath is a chance to rewrite the script,
To dance with fate's jokes, to allow life to flip.
So let's breathe in the laughter, breathe out all the doom,
In this circus of wonder, we'll make our hearts bloom.

The Heart's Silent Inventory

In the backroom of my heart,
I sift through dreams and fears.
I check for joy on aisle three,
    Find only misplaced tears.

The shelves are stocked with old regrets,
And prices marked with dust.
I try to find a funny joke,
    Just end up in a rust.

A cart of hopes rolls down the lane,
With snacks of bittersweet.
But every time I reach for bliss,
    There's nothing left to eat.

So I put my faith in coupons rare,
And laugh when they expire.
For in this store of fleeting thoughts,
    I still can't find desire.

Threads of Purpose Unraveled

In life's vast fabric, threads unwind,
With each pull, a giggle's found.
My needle's lost, it's quite the mess,
Stitches frayed all around.

A tapestry hangs on the wall,
Colors bright, I once did boast.
Now it's a patchwork of silly tales,
Where I forgot the toast.

Each fray a laugh, each knot a smile,
As I weave my days away.
Yet here I sit, threads in a tangle,
Sewing up yesterday.

For every goal I thought I'd hit,
Fell flat like soda pop.
And in this funny little weave,
I may just never stop.

Lost in the Aisles of Existence

Navigating life's big store,
I misread all the signs.
I tripped on aisles of hope and joy,
And dropped my clever rhymes.

Behind the chips of human woes,
I found a row of dreams.
The sales clerk said, 'They all run out,'
I think that's just his schemes.

The checkout line's a great big laugh,
Where waiting turns to play.
With cart full of old silly thoughts,
I want to leave today.

So if you find the meaning there,
In stock or on the shelf,
Just trade it for a quick dessert,
Or borrow it from self.

In Search of Forgotten Words

I wander through a crossword maze,
Each clue a little tease.
I search for words that rhyme with hope,
But end up saying 'cheese'.

In dusty tomes of tangled thoughts,
I flip through pages thick.
But all the verbs have run away,
I'm left with just a tick.

Synonyms of joy feel lost,
While laughter fills the void.
Yet all I grasp are puns and quirks,
And I can't help but be annoyed.

So as I search for clever phrases,
To make the void feel bright,
I find the best poetic lines,
Are often just pure light.

Labels of Longing

In aisles of hope, I search with glee,
For products of joy that used to be.
With labels that fade, they slip away,
Leaving me puzzled at the end of the day.

I chase after dreams like a lost little pup,
Only to find they're all sold out, what a hiccup!
My cart is empty, my list is long,
I should've known 'out of stock' was wrong!

I peeked at the shelf labeled 'satisfaction,'
But the stock was thin, a sad reaction.
If only my heart came with a return policy,
I'd swap my desires for some good quality.

Oh, the items I want, they evaded my spree,
As I walk home, I can only just see.
Next time I'll check the aisle for delight,
Fingers crossed for a sale to ignite my night!

The Void Between Now and Never

I stand in the gap, a comedic scene,
Between fleeting moments, where's been?
The clock ticks slowly, a joke on me,
Where's the laughter? Oh, let it be!

Time's out of stock, like a funny old play,
I waited for wisdom - it went astray.
Each tick brings a chuckle I can't describe,
It's a circus act now, I'm losing my vibe.

Now I'm caught in a loop, the cosmic jest,
With each second passing, I'm truly the best!
But the universe chuckles with stars in a wink,
As I stand in the void—wait, is that a pink drink?

Between now and never, it's all a good joke,
I'll gather the laughs 'fore I choke.
With every mad tick, I'll dance with flair,
Who knew that 'never' could bring such air?

An Empty Cart in Aisle Seven

My cart is hollow, it echoes my plight,
In aisle seven, where dreams take flight.
I browse through the shelves of all I desire,
Only to find the good stuff is dire.

Oh look, there's hope, but it's out of stock,
I check the next aisle, that didn't rock.
Humor me now, it's getting absurd,
I'm shopping for wisdom, have you heard?

I try to find laughter on that shiny rack,
But the jokes are scarce, they've all gone slack.
An empty cart, it's a paradox grand,
As I wander through thoughts I don't understand.

A store of my dreams, all boxed up tight,
If only the checkout could bring me delight.
But with every item, I'm left with a laugh,
As I roll out the door with my comical path.

The Warehouse of Wishes

In a warehouse snug with dust and delight,
I search for my wishes, but they're not in sight.
Each shelf I climb is a ladder of dreams,
Yet all I encounter are empty, lost beams.

I thought I'd find happiness tomes with flair,
But instead I find cobwebs, I must declare.
The managers chuckle from high above,
It seems wish-making's a game not of love.

A sign on the wall reads, 'Stock running low,'
Should I barter with fate? I'm feeling the flow.
With humor I bargain for some silly jest,
Only to leave with a ghost as my guest.

So here I stand, in this whimsical place,
With racks full of laughter, but no saving grace.
Is the punchline out of stock, or just misplaced?
In this warehouse of wishes, nothing's erased!

Barcodes Without Value

In a shop where dreams are sold,
I scanned my heart, only to be told,
'No discount here, your hopes are spent,'
A label stuck, but none was meant.

I tried to trade a smile or two,
But they just laughed, said, 'Who are you?'
With empty shelves that gleam and glow,
I left with nothing, just a woe.

A price tag marked in joyful jest,
'Clearance sale on feeling blessed!'
But every thought was out of stock,
Like socks that vanish from the clock.

So now I roam this endless aisle,
With jokes in hand and empty style,
I'd bargain hard but can't decide,
What's really worth the crazy ride?

Silence in the Marketplace

The market buzzes, oh so grand,
Yet all I hear is silence planned,
Where echoes dance on empty shelves,
And laughter's lost, it's hiding, dwells.

I shout for joy, they look confused,
'Where's the party? We've been bruised!'
A silent sale on wit and cheer,
They price the joy, but none appear.

Tick-tock goes the shopping cart,
As cost of giggles fades apart,
With purchase smiles, I try to trade,
But all I find is silence made.

So here I stand with empty bags,
Collecting sighs like old rags,
In a marketplace where fun's out quoted,
I bid farewell, slightly corroded.

Ghosts of Unmade Choices

In the isles where options flee,
I found an aisle labeled 'Let it be,'
With ghostly whispers of missed delight,
Ah, the choices haunt me every night.

'Pick a flavor, any one!'
I picked too late, the battle's won,
Each step I take on this spooky floor,
Breathless echoes shout, 'Choose, choose more!'

I grab a can labeled 'What if?'
But opened it found only a tiff,
With every chance now marked as loot,
The ghosts just giggle and point, tooot!

So here I stroll with chuckles grim,
Haunted by choices, chances slim,
In the market of 'what could've been,'
My cart rolls on, in humorous spin.

The Cost of Absence

I wandered through this empty space,
Where absence has a hefty grace,
'In stock, we have the things you lack,'
I just rolled my eyes, it's a hack!

With zero courage to make a find,
A price tag mocks my racing mind,
'What's the cost of a missing grin?'
They shrugged their shoulders, 'Let's begin.'

'Special today! Heart not included,'
As laughter echoes, my hopes eluded,
With aisles of thoughts I cannot gain,
It's all a joke, an endless game.

Yet here in absence, I might just see,
The funny side of 'come shop with me,'
For deep inside this empty scene,
I'm rich in jokes, if not in sheen.

Dreams on a Faded Label

In an attic filled with dust and dreams,
I found a label with faded seams.
It promised joy, a prize to seek,
But all it had was a squeaky speak.

I shook it hard, gave it a spin,
Hoping for treasure, but got a grin.
A sock, a spoon, and a rubber duck,
Maybe that's just my kind of luck!

I tossed the dreams like yesterday's bread,
In hopes they'd sprout in someone's head.
But they rolled away, with a laugh and a wink,
I guess that wisdom is best left to think.

So here's to labels that lead us astray,
Wrapping our hopes in peculiar play.
For when we seek joy tangled in threads,
We find it in sock puppets dancing instead!

The Quest for Unwritten Chapters

With a pen in hand, I sought the script,
Of unwritten tales I'd zealously grip.
But every page was empty and stark,
Overgrown with weeds, no light or spark.

I strolled through plots like a confused fool,
Stepping on chapters that once were cool.
A cat in a hat said, 'Try a new twist!'
So I scribbled a line—did I get the gist?

The pages yelled back, 'We're all but a jest!'
You think you're the hero? Oh, what a fest!
So maybe the quest for the unwritten glance,
Is just a long journey where we prance.

A tale to tell, with laughter in tow,
In every blank space where wild ideas grow.
So I'll raise my glass to the stories in thought,
Embrace the chaos and give it a shot!

Echoes of Untold Stories

In the alley where whispers dwell,
Echoes of stories refuse to tell.
I listened close, with a crick in my neck,
But all I found was a laughing speck.

A dog barked loudly, 'What's the deal?'
The echoes chuckled, 'Don't take the wheel!'
They danced and twirled, like shadows in place,
Reminding me laughter is hard to chase.

I grabbed a pencil, sketched on the wall,
But the echoes just giggled at my scribbling call.
Perhaps these tales are too grand to share,
Or just a reminder to lighten the air.

So I shout to the echoes, 'Let's spin a yarn!'
They replied, 'Only if you bring the charm!'
Here's to the stories that we never unveil,
Maybe that's when we will truly prevail!

When Clarity Hides Behind the Clouds

The sun peeks out, then pulls away,
Leaving me puzzled on this sunny day.
With clarity lost in a fluffy maze,
I squint and shout, 'Where are the rays?'

A cloud chuckles, 'Oh, take a break!
You'll find your answers in fog, for heaven's sake!'
I sip my tea, wait for the light,
But it plays hide and seek, a charming fright.

The wind blows softly, teasing my mind,
In every shadow, confusion I find.
I chase ideas, but they dance away,
'Tis just the weather, who needs dismay?

So here I stand beneath this grand sky,
Embracing the clouds, letting dreams fly.
A funny twist in this hazy plight,
Sometimes the fun is in not being right!

www.ingramcontent.com/pod-product-compliance
Lightning Source LLC
Chambersburg PA
CBHW071842160426
43209CB00003B/382